Pebble® Plus

The Calendar

How Long Is a YEAR?

by Claire Clark

Consulting Editor: Gail Saunders-Smith, PhD

CAPSTONE PRESS
a capstone imprint

Pebble Plus is published by Capstone Press,
1710 Roe Crest Drive, North Mankato, Minnesota 56003.
www.capstonepub.com

 Books published by Capstone Press are manufactured with paper
containing at least 10 percent post-consumer waste.

Library of Congress Cataloging-in-Publication Data
Clark, Claire, 1973–
  How long is a year? / by Claire Clark.
    p. cm. — (Pebble plus. The calendar)
  Summary: "Simple text and photos explain a year as a unit of time and Earth's orbit of the sun"—Provided
by publisher.
  Includes bibliographical references and index.
  ISBN 978-1-4296-7594-9 (library binding)
  ISBN 978-1-4296-7901-5 (paperback)
  1. Year—Juvenile literature. 2. Earth—Rotation—Juvenile literature. 3. Earth—Orbit—Juvenile literature.
4. Time measurements—Juvenile literature. I. Title.
  QB209.5.C5835 2012
  529'.2—dc23   2011025048

Editorial Credits
Kristen Mohn, editor; Bobbie Nuytten, designer; Marcie Spence, media researcher; Marcy Morin, studio scheduler;
    Sarah Schuette, photo stylist; Kathy McColley, production specialist

Photo Credits
Capstone Studio: Karon Dubke, cover (boy), 1 (bottom), 5, 7, 9, 11, 15, 17, 19, 21; Shutterstock: Dr_Flash, cover
    (Earth), 1 (top), Nixx Photography, cover (space), Smit, 13

Note to Parents and Teachers

The Calendar series supports national science and social studies standards related to time.
This book describes and illustrates what makes a year. The images support early readers in
understanding the text. The repetition of words and phrases helps early readers learn new
words. This book also introduces early readers to subject-specific vocabulary words, which are
defined in the Glossary section. Early readers may need assistance to read some words and to
use the Table of Contents, Glossary, Read More, Internet Sites, and Index sections of the book.

Printed in the United States of America in North Mankato, Minnesota.

102011   006405CGS12

Table of Contents

What Is a Year? 4

What Makes a Year? 8

What Lasts a Year? 14

Glossary 22

Read More 23

Internet Sites 23

Index 24

What Is a Year?

Today is Tia's birthday!

She will be seven years old

for 12 months.

That's 52 weeks.

That's also 365 days.

A year lasts from January

through December.

Every year we start

a new calendar.

What Makes a Year?

Earth travels around the sun once every 12 months. Long ago people named that period of time a year.

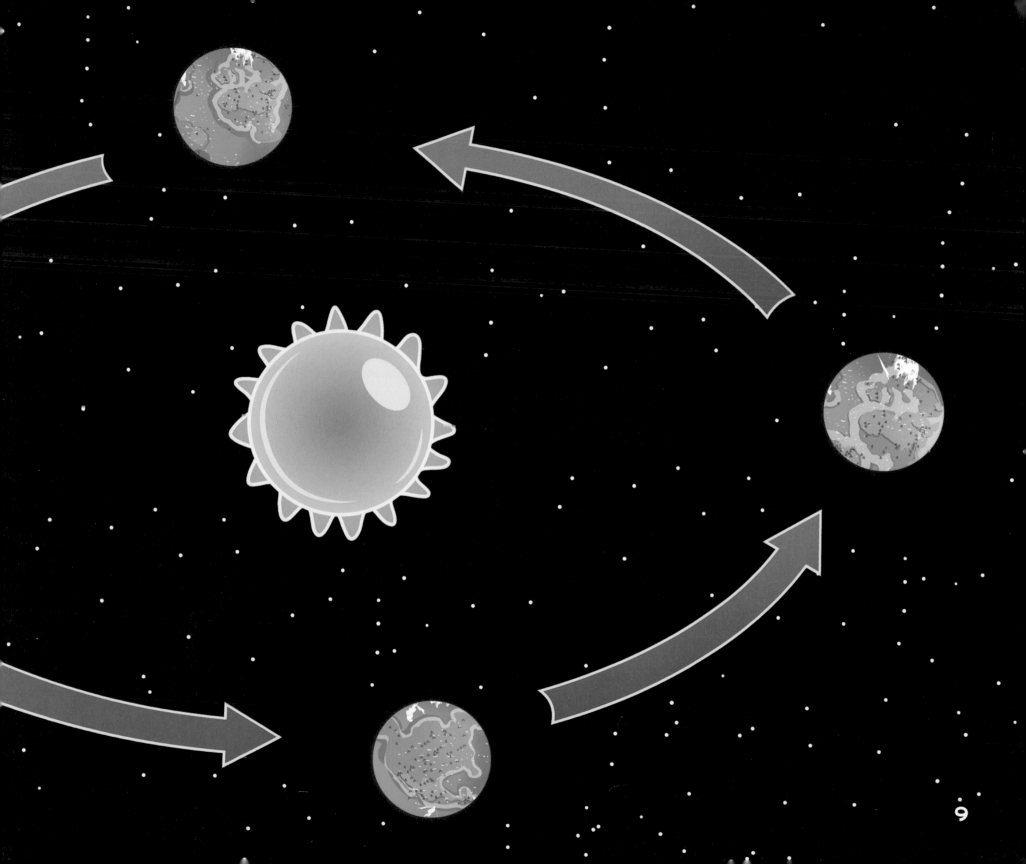

Earth is tilted to one side.

It spins on its axis.

While Earth spins,

it circles the sun.

As Earth goes around, different parts of it face the sun. The sun warms those parts more than the other parts. This causes our seasons.

13

What Lasts a Year?

Your age lasts a year.

This year Tia is seven.

Next year she'll be eight.

Your grade in school lasts a year. This year Tia is in first grade. Next year she'll be in second grade.

In a year children grow.

Each year Tia might grow

2 inches (5 centimeters) taller!

In a year you can learn

many things.

This year Tia will learn

to ride a bike.

What will you learn?

Glossary

axis—a real or imaginary line through the center of an object, around which the object turns

calendar—a chart that shows all of the days, weeks, and months in a year

season—one of the four parts of the year; winter, spring, summer, and fall are seasons

tilt—an angle or lean; not straight

Read More

Adamson, Thomas K., and Heather Adamson. *How Do You Measure Time?* Measure It! Mankato, Minn.: Capstone Press, 2011.

Scheunemann, Pam. *Time to Learn about Seasons & Years.* Edina, Minn.: ABDO Pub., 2008.

Steffora, Tracey. *Seasons of the Year.* Measuring Time. Chicago: Heinemann Library, 2011.

Internet Sites

FactHound offers a safe, fun way to find Internet sites related to this book. All of the sites on FactHound have been researched by our staff.

Here's all you do:

Visit *www.facthound.com*

Type in this code: 9781429675949

 Check out projects, games and lots more at **www.capstonekids.com**

Index

age, 14

axis, 10

calendar, 6

days, 4

Earth, 8, 10, 12

grade, 16

growth, 18

months, 4, 6, 8

seasons, 12

sun, 8, 10, 12

weeks, 4

Word Count: 186
Grade: 1
Early-Intervention Level: 19